VINCE

C000213869

INTRODUCTION

This book is about a very exciting period in Britain's history. Following the collapse of the Roman Empire, Britain was settled and dominated by pagan Germanic peoples. Missionaries arrived to convert many to Christianity. Its people survived numerous Viking invasions and internal fighting and finally a single nation emerged.

We discover that Anglo-Saxon society was not a 'dark' period in our history, but one of amazing achievement. The only English king to be called 'Great' lived in these times. Much of our cultural heritage, laws and our language began here. If that isn't enough, we have in recent years unearthed the most stunning buried treasure! The finds at Sutton Hoo and the Staffordshire Hoard represent the finest craftsmanship in Europe at that time. Arguably no period in our nation's history is more important in our understanding of where the English people came from.

CONTENTS

	Page
PART 1 AD 410-600	
Pagan Britain	4
PART 2 AD 600-800	
Christian Kingdoms	6
King Raedwald	8
The Staffordshire Hoard	10
Arts and Crafts	11
The Venerable Bede	12
PART 3 AD 800-1066	
The Coming of the Vikings	14
King Alfred 'The Great'	16
Viking Rulers	18
The Norman Invasion	20
Giant Anglo-Saxon Word Search	22
Timeline and Glossary	23

Written & illustrated by William Webb
Front cover illustration by Les Ives
Published by Colour Heroes Ltd © 2011
Print reference number 36287/03/11

PART 1 AD 410-600
Pagan Britain

As the power of the Roman Empire weakened, the Angles, Saxons and Jutes sent raiding parties to the Roman province of 'Britannia'. The Romans built forts along the 'Saxon Shore', which housed ships and troops to defend themselves against these attacks.

The Roman Empire was weakened by in-fighting and foreign invasions. By AD 410 the Emperor Honorius told the people of Britain that they would now have to defend themselves. Roman troops never returned to the province and Rome itself fell to Goth invaders in the same year.

King Arthur and the British Resistance
The Roman province of Britain was inhabited by a small population of Romano-British peoples with a mainly Celtic background. When the Romans left Britain power fell into the hands of local warlords, one of which may have been the legendary King Arthur. Arthur and other Romano-British leaders put up fierce resistance to repeated Anglo-Saxon invasions, winning a major victory at the Battle of Mount Badon in AD 500. However, it was only a matter of time before Britain was overrun by these unwelcome invaders.

The Anglo-Saxons were a Germanic people and were not new to Britain, as many had served in Britain in the Roman army. When the Picts started attacking from the north, Anglo-Saxon leaders Hengist and Horsa were invited to help defend England against them. They were given land in the east of England as a reward, but they rebelled and the Anglo-Saxon settlement of Britain began.

The Beginning of the 'Dark Ages'
The first Anglo-Saxons travelled up English rivers in small boats and settled on the land. They pushed the Romano-British locals further west and mixed with them, or enslaved them, no one knows exactly which. As a result, Christianity and Roman culture largely vanished from the areas settled by the pagan invaders.

> **Did You Know?**
> The name 'Saxon' originates from the dagger the early Saxons carried in a leather sheath, which was called a *seax*, pronounced 'sax'.

The Anglo-Saxons Settle
When they arrived the Anglo-Saxons found run-down farms and empty Roman towns. They recycled materials left by the Romans and found land to farm in the river valleys, sharing it out amongst their followers. They lived in small villages, each of which had a tribal leader. Some leaders became kings. Their noble warriors were called 'thanes'. Thanes were usually given land by the King in return for their loyalty and service. The thane allowed farmers, or 'churls' to farm the land and in return the churls fought for him, paid him rent and worked his land. The Roman way of life, which was centred in towns and villas, had now vanished and the new 'Germanic' way of life took over. By AD 600 a number of independent kingdoms emerged and by AD 700 the great kingdom of Mercia was established (see page 6).

The English Language
The Anglo-Saxons spoke 'Germanic', or 'Old English', this replaced the Latin language of the Romano-British aristocracy and the Celtic language of the lower classes. Celtic language survived in Cornwall, Wales and Britanny in France, which was named after Britain. This is where many Romano-British people had moved to. The language of Britanny, 'Breton', is similar to Welsh and Cornish.

A PAGAN WEEK
The Germanic gods of the Anglo-Saxons gave their names to days of the week:

Tuesday	=	**Tiw's Day**
Wednesday	=	**Woden** or **Odin's Day**
Thursday	=	**Thunor** or **Thor's Day**
Friday	=	**Frig** or **Freya's Day.**

The goddess Eostre gave her name to 'Easter' and her symbols were the hare and the egg, from where we get Easter eggs and bunnies!

THE INVADERS

Angles from southern Denmark settled in East Anglia, 'East Angles'.

Saxons from North Germany and Holland settled in the south of England. They formed the kingdoms of Sussex, 'South Saxons', Wessex, 'West Saxons', Essex, 'East Saxons' and Middlesex 'Middle Saxons'.

The Jutes from Jutland in northern Denmark settled mainly in Kent, Hampshire and the Isle of Wight.

Frisians and Franks joined the invasions.

Make a piece of A4 paper look old by tearing the edges to make them uneven. Now dye it with a used wet teabag. When dry, make a map of Anglo-Saxon lands, you can copy the one below, or use an atlas. Decorate the sea with Saxon ships and then gently crumple the paper to give it an antique look. Maps in those days were not accurate, so don't worry if yours isn't!

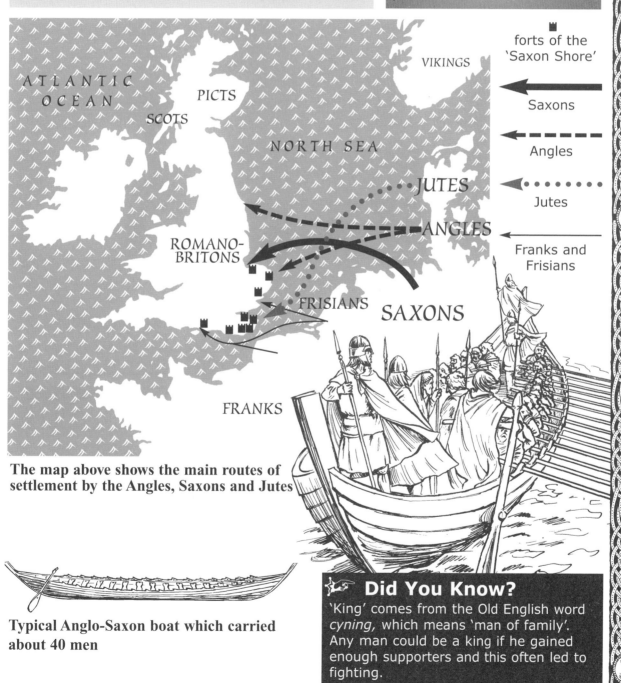

The map above shows the main routes of settlement by the Angles, Saxons and Jutes

Typical Anglo-Saxon boat which carried about 40 men

Did You Know?
'King' comes from the Old English word *cyning,* which means 'man of family'. Any man could be a king if he gained enough supporters and this often led to fighting.

PART 2 AD 600-800
Christian Kingdoms

"At the feast of Christmas last more than 10,000 English are reported to have been baptised." **So wrote Pope Gregory I in a letter in AD 598. Christianity, once threatened with extinction in England, was returning and would completely change pagan Anglo-Saxon society forever.**

In AD 596 Pope Gregory sent St Augustine and a group of 40 monks to England to convert the Anglo-Saxons. Whilst travelling across France they began to get cold feet and returned to the Pope, hoping he would call off the mission! The Pope sent them back the following year and they landed in Kent in AD 597. The King of Kent, Aethelberht, or Ethelbert was a pagan, but his wife Queen Bertha was already a Christian. At Easter in AD 601 Augustine baptised Aethelberht and his court. With the conversion of the most powerful king in England, Christianity spread quickly throughout the land. Within a hundred years, Christian monasteries in northern England had produced magnificent 'illuminated' books like the Lindisfarne Gospels. In the 8th century Anglo-Saxon missionaries took the gospel to the Germans.

The Growth of the Church

Christianity spread downward from the Kings and their courts to the people. Pagan practices and cemeteries were gradually abandoned, particularly the burial of possessions with the dead. Missionaries brought the art of writing with them and a new Anglo-Saxon script developed. History could be recorded for the first time in Britain (see page 12) and an 'English' style of art developed.

King Aethelberht was the first to have his laws written down. Stories such as Beowulf (see page 11), which were traditionally passed down orally, could now be recorded. Trade with the continent flourished, technology advanced and coinage, which had disappeared with the Romans, was used again. Towns, once common in the Roman Empire, began to grow up around churches and monasteries, as the monks needed craftsmen and traders. Monks provided the only education available, but it was only for the privileged few. Kings and the nobility grew in power, wealth and influence, as did the power of the church.

Five Kingdoms

Five kingdoms dominated England, they were Kent, Wessex, Northumbria (which means 'north of the River Humber'), East Anglia and Mercia. They fought each other and at times one king would grow powerful enough to be 'overlord' and rule the whole country.

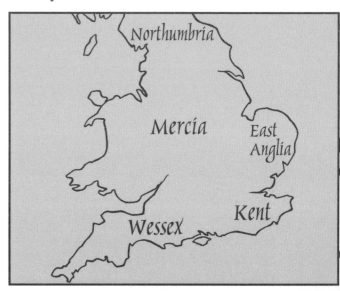

🐾 Did You Know?
The word 'gospel' comes from the Old English word *godspel* which means 'good story' or 'good news'.

What's in a Name?
Anglo-Saxon words can still be found in modern place-names. Here is a list of some of them:

burn = stream

bury = fort or large town

combe = small valley

cot = small house

dun, den, dene = hill

feld, field = field

ford = river crossing

ham = settlement

ley, ly, lea, leigh = clearing in a wood

mere = lake

tun, ton = farm/village

wick, wich, wic = farm

worth = land enclosed by a hedge

Look at a map and find some towns near you which have Anglo-Saxon place-names.

Anglo-Saxon Society

Usually people spent their lives in the position they were born into. At the top of society was the King who was in charge of the thanes.

The thanes were in charge of several villages.

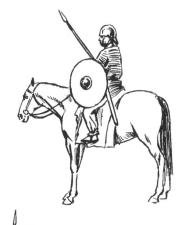

Each village of two, or three families had a headman from the churls whose family had special status.

Below them came the other families who were ordinary small farmers and peasants.

Lastly, there were slaves who were prisoners captured in war, criminals or those who were so poor that they had to sell themselves into slavery.

Daily Life at West Stow in Suffolk

There were many changes in everyday life during the 600 years of Anglo-Saxon settlement. Archaeology provides us with clues about the daily life of people living in an early Anglo-Saxon village. The site excavated and now reconstructed at West Stow in Suffolk, shows us that the early Anglo-Saxons lived in wooden houses with thatched roofs. The houses had small windows without glass. Although they had fires and a hearth they did not have a chimney, so their single rooms could get very smoky! One family had several buildings for different uses, such as weaving, storage, living and sleeping, just like the rooms in a modern house today.

Villages like West Stow, which was in use around AD 450-650, were small and normally consisted of two or three family groups, each with six or seven houses. There would have been a hall for meetings and feasts. They did not have wooden fences, or a ditch for protection against enemies, as this came later. At first people made everything they needed for themselves, but gradually they became specialist craftsmen.

Land was farmed in long strips, so that the difficult job of turning a plough and oxen around did not have to be done too often. They shared the strips, so that no-one had the best land. They grew wheat, rye, barley, oats, peas, beans and lentils.

Towns, or 'wics', did not develop until around AD 600. The early towns like Hamwic, which is now Southampton and Gipeswic, now Ipswich were often sited on the coast. This ensured the best use of traders and craftsmen, who set up stalls nearby, whilst their customers built new houses.

Visit the West Stow website at www.weststow.org

A typical early Anglo-Saxon village

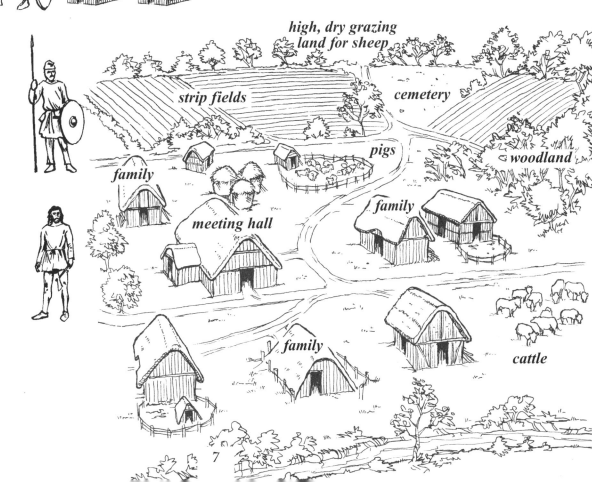

high, dry grazing land for sheep

strip fields

cemetery

pigs

woodland

family

family

meeting hall

family

cattle

King Raedwald

In about AD 625 a great warrior, or king was buried at Sutton Hoo near Woodbridge in Suffolk, in a pagan earth mound. For over 1,300 years he lay undisturbed, surrounded by glittering treasures of unsurpassable quality.

In 1939, just before the outbreak of war in Europe, the impression of a huge buried ship was found in one of the twenty mounds at Sutton Hoo. It had survived without being looted, unlike some of the other mounds, as it had been buried deeper. A series of excavations revealed many treasures and another buried ship. During World War II the finds were stored by the British Museum in the London Underground for safety.

What was Discovered?
In the huge ship there was a chamber containing the possessions of an important man. A jewelled shield, a coat of mail armour, a long sword with a jewelled hilt, a superbly decorated helmet with eyebrows, moustache and a bird-shaped nose, a whetstone resembling a sceptre, an iron standard, ornamented horns for drinking out of and other treasures, including coins, valuable cloaks and cloth hangings. Some items had been imported from the Mediterranean. The red garnet stones used in many of the decorations had been brought all the way from India!

Who was the Man in the Grave?
Many people believe the man buried in the ship at Sutton Hoo is King Raedwald. He was the most important man of his day and had gathered all of the English kingdoms under his influence.

King Aethelberht of Kent was the most powerful King of his day and had converted to Christianity (see page 6). Raedwald was only a junior king at this time and he went to Kent to be baptised. He returned to his home in East Anglia, but his Queen, whose name we do not know, told him not to give up the old gods completely. So he kept a temple with altars to the pagan gods and to Christ and steadily he built up his power.

In about AD 616 Aethelberht died. He had protected a prince called Edwin who had fled from the King of Northumbria. Now Edwin went to Raedwald in East Anglia for help, but the King of Northumbria offered bribes and threats to Raedwald and asked him to hand over Edwin. Raedwald's Queen, who seemed to be quite a remarkable woman, counselled him not to sell his honour for money by betraying the ancient obligations to look after a guest. So, instead Raedwald marched north and killed the King of Northumbria and put Edwin on the Northumbrian throne! Raedwald lost his own son in the battle, but he was now the most powerful king of England. Edwin heard the gospel at Raedwald's court and after the death of Raedwald in about AD 625, he became a Christian and married into the ruling families of Kent and East Anglia, defeating the pagan rulers of Mercia.

Is Sutton Hoo Unique?
Another ship burial was discovered a few miles away in 1862 at a place called Snape. The only other part of the world where this type of burial has been found is in Sweden. Many of the Sutton Hoo treasures were made by Swedish craftsmen. The custom of burying important people underneath their ships and covering the site with an earth mound was common in Scandinavia, where it lasted for about 400 years.

A PLACE OF EXECUTION

Curiously, the site at Sutton Hoo was also used for executions. Several impressions in the soil have been found of men and women who were beheaded or hanged, possibly from gallows. Their bones have long since rotted away, but the remains of post holes have been found.

Sutton 'Hoo'?

'Hoo' is the same as *haugh* in Old English and means 'a high place' such as the top of a hill. Not all the mounds have been excavated, so who knows what other secrets lie waiting to be uncovered at Sutton Hoo?

An important person has died today and they are to be buried in the same way as King Raedwald. What kind of things should go into his or her burial chamber?

8

Buried Treasure

What Else is Buried There?

One mound contained the burial of an important woman. Another mound contained a warrior buried with his weapons and possessions, including some lamb chops in a kit-bag! His horse had been sacrificed and buried in a mound next to him. There are also the remains of people in metal urns who had been cremated with other types of animals. These people were probably related to Raedwald's family, the Wuffinga's, which means 'Wolf's People'.

How Big Was the Boat?

At 27 metres, it could accommodate up to 30 oarsmen. It was not new when it was buried, as it has evidence of many repairs.

Visit the Sutton Hoo website at www.nationaltrust.org.uk/suttonhoo

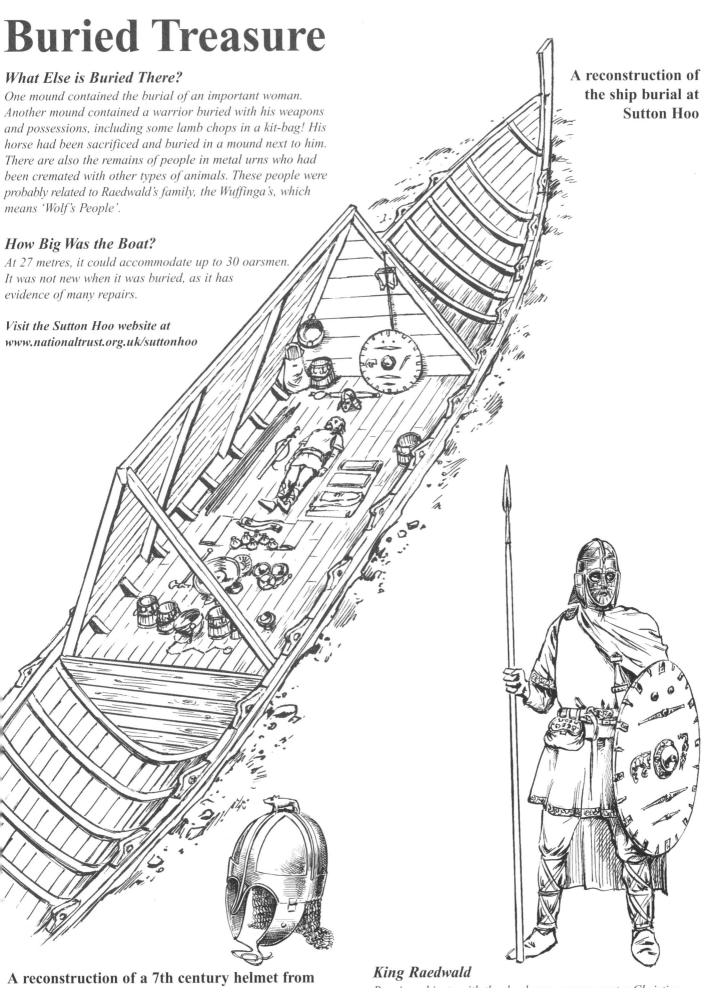

A reconstruction of the ship burial at Sutton Hoo

A reconstruction of a 7th century helmet from the grave of another important Anglo-Saxon warrior. His helmet carries a model of a boar, a pagan symbol mentioned in the epic poem 'Beowulf' (see page 11).

King Raedwald

Burying objects with the dead was a pagan, not a Christian custom, and King Raedwald's body was not found in the ship. However, it could have disappeared in the acid sandy soil. This is a reconstruction of what the King may have looked like dressed in the items found in the ship.

9

The Staffordshire Hoard

The first pieces of the Staffordshire Hoard were found in early July 2009 by Terry Herbert, using a metal detector. He reported his find and archaeologists then excavated the site for four weeks in July and August.

By the time the dig finished the hoard contained over 3,400 objects and fragments totalling over 5 kilos of gold and 1½ kilos of silver, making it the largest hoard of treasure ever found in Britain. The hoard was officially declared to be treasure and the Birmingham Museum and Art Gallery and the Potteries Museum and Art Gallery, Stoke-on-Trent, jointly raised £3,285,000 to buy it. You can see pieces from the hoard on display at both of these museums.

How old is the hoard?
The hoard is still being studied, but archaeologists think that it was buried somewhere between 650 and 700 AD. They have arrived at this date by comparing some of the objects in the hoard with those already known from other sites.

What is in the hoard?
The Staffordshire Hoard is very unusual because it seems to be largely made up of military equipment. It includes pieces from the handles of nearly a hundred swords, but not the sword blades. These were probably given new handles and reused. The hoard probably included part of a helmet very like the helmet from Sutton Hoo. There are also three Christian items, including a large cross that has been folded up to go in the hoard, a cross that would have been worn around the neck of a bishop, or another important churchman, and a strip of gold inscribed with a text from the Bible in Latin (and includes two spelling mistakes!).

Who hid the hoard, and why?
We simply don't know the answer to these questions yet. Perhaps we never will, but there are lots of theories. Was it loot taken from dead warriors after a battle or battles? Was it stolen and hidden? Was it left as an offering to the pagan gods? Was it a royal treasure hidden to keep it safe from enemies? What do you think it might be?

Write your own story telling us the tale of the Staffordshire Hoard.

Detailed Decoration
Many of the objects in the hoard are decorated with what is known as 'animal interlace' decoration. This means that the decoration is made up of animals whose bodies curl around each other, sometimes in very complicated patterns. The little gold plaque below has a simple example of this decoration, with two animals, each consisting of a head, a body and a foot, biting each others' body.

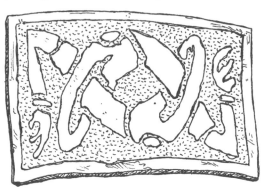

Below is one of the most important pieces in the hoard. It is a gold cross that was originally decorated with red, semi-precious stones called garnets. The mounts containing the garnets were taken off the cross and all but one of them was removed. The garnet that was left had been broken and was probably left for that reason. The cross was then folded up and the mounts pushed inside it, which is how it was found. If you look closely, you can see more animal interlace decoration on the cross.

Visit the Staffordshire Hoard website at
www.staffordshirehoard.org.uk/artefacts

Arts & Crafts

Christian missionaries introduced books to the Anglo-Saxons as a method of communication and an object of devotion and decoration. Writing was to have a big impact on Anglo-Saxon society, much like the internet has changed our modern world today.

Now kings could keep records and write down their laws. Across the country different laws could be standardised and taxes could be recorded. For the first time events could be written down in books, such as the 'Ecclesiastical History of the English People' written by a monk called Bede (see page 12). There were schools for priests and monks. Young men were taught Greek, Latin, religion and law.

At first most writing was in Latin, but during the reign of King Alfred (see page 16), the 'vernacular' or common Anglo-Saxon language of the people was increasingly used.

The Bard
A popular form of entertainment was story-telling. At Sutton Hoo a lyre was discovered in a beaver skin. Bards would play the lyre and recite long poems about great heroes. This taught lessons about how to be brave and generous. Imagine life without television or cinema, bards were just as important to the Anglo-Saxons. Most people could not write, so these stories were memorised and passed down orally. The poems did not rhyme and were characterised by alliteration. They were told at feasts, or special celebrations in the meeting hall.

'Beowulf' and Why it is Important
The oldest surviving tale is called 'Beowulf'. This epic poem tells of a Swedish prince who travelled to the palace of a Danish king. Beowulf is a superman with the strength of thirty warriors. He defeats a bloodthirsty monster called Grendel, who had been snatching warriors as they slept from the Danish King's hall. Beowulf kills the monster's mother in her lair, but he dies whilst killing a dragon. This poem is over 3,000 lines long and was not written down until about the tenth century.

Beowulf is important because it tells us about aspects of Anglo-Saxon life, which history and archaeology cannot, particularly their thoughts and feelings. The village in the story sounds like West Stow.

Metalwork
The Anglo-Saxons were highly skilled craftsmen. The goldsmith and jeweller who made the sword, belt-fittings and other items found at Sutton Hoo were amongst the best in Northern Europe. They combined animal and geometric designs with Roman styles to make King Raedwald look like a Roman emperor. The use of human faces and animals in metalwork may have had a magical purpose. The boar may have been a power symbol and was often used on helmets.

Wood and Bone
The Anglo-Saxons used the pole-lathe to make wooden cups, bowls, furniture and tool handles. Bone and antlers were shaped into keys, pins, needles, combs and handles, as well as for decorating products.

Women's Crafts
Women spun and wove wool and linen to make clothes. They had a wide range of weaving techniques. They wove baskets from willow twigs and made traps for fish and eels.

Other Crafts
Leatherworkers made everything from shoes to horse harnesses. Pottery was mass produced in the growing towns, where the potters wheel and kilns replaced the simple coil method of pot making. Monks from the continent brought building and carving in stone to England. The first stone buildings were churches and monasteries, which had a new feature, the tower.

Before their conversion to Christianity, Anglo-Saxons used runes for writing. Write out a secret message in runes using the alphabet below as a guide.

Runes

f u th o r k g w h n i j h p x s t b e n g m l d œ a æ y ea

The Venerable Bede

Most of our written information about Britain after the Romans comes from Bede, *'the father of English history'*. His life and work was so important that the period from AD 600-800 is often called the 'Age of Bede'.

Bede was a Christian scholar, teacher and writer. He lived from AD 673 to AD 735 and he wrote many books, including his most famous one called 'The Ecclesiastical History of the English People'. He wrote books explaining the bible, and books on astronomy, maths, nature and the reckoning of time.

A Monk of Wearmouth-Jarrow

Little is known of Bede's early life, but we do know that he was born in Northumbria. At the age of seven his family entrusted him to Benedict Biscop, who was the founder of the monastery at Wearmouth. A year later more land was granted to Benedict and the Jarrow part of the monastery was founded. Despite it being in two places Wearmouth-Jarrow was a single monastery and Bede spent his whole life there. He was ordained as a priest at the age of thirty.

His Work

Bede was the first person ever to compile a history of what had happened in England. Before his work, history was based on stories of what people could remember. At the monastery there were many books from all over Christian Europe and Bede began researching what had happened in England, using all of the evidence he could find. This is the way a modern historian works, but it was very new in the 8th century. It is because of Bede's work that we can learn a great deal about life in Anglo-Saxon times.

Bede was a well respected scholar whose books were used for teaching. Since his death he has been greatly admired and in 1899 it was decided that the 27th May would officially be celebrated as the feast day of the Venerable Bede.

Visit the Bede's World website at www.bedesworld.co.uk

The Lindisfarne Gospels

Cut off from the mainland by high tides twice a day, Lindisfarne can feel quite remote. For this reason it was an ideal base for 7th century Irish missionaries, led by St Aidan, to establish a monastery here in AD 635. The island became known as Holy Island and the monks began to convert northern Anglo-Saxons from paganism to Christianity.

From the 670s Lindisfarne was the home of St Cuthbert, the most famous of its monk-bishops. Because of Cuthbert the community at Lindisfarne was very well-known and it became a centre for Christian learning. Between 700 and 725 one of the most famous pieces of medieval art was produced there, the Lindisfarne Gospels.

Beautifully produced by hand, they are a copy of the Latin New Testament. The 258 pages would have needed at least 150 calf skins in perfect condition to make the parchment on which the texts are written.

After careful study and using information that we know about the Gospels we can tell that it was created by one man called Eadfrith. If you have a chance to visit Lindisfarne Priory you will see what a talented artist Eadfrith was.

Visit the Lindisfarne Priory website at www.english-heritage. org.uk/daysout/properties/lindisfarne-priory/

Illuminated Writing

Draw a large letter and decorate it with animals, dragons, people and flowers. Colour it in using bright colours.

This illuminated initial is from a book of Psalms and shows David killing Goliath

It's your life!

Write a brief history of your life. What evidence will you need to gather to make sure it is an accurate account? Who will you need to talk to?

Law and Order

The Anglo-Saxons introduced the system of trial by a twelve-man jury. Trials took place in local courts. The most common crimes were cattle stealing and theft. If caught, people would be hanged, whipped or have their little fingers cut off. The King and his advisers, a 'witan', presided over very serious cases.

Bloodprice

If a person hurt or killed someone else they had to pay his family money. It was called the 'bloodprice' or 'wergeld'. It was introduced to stop constant fighting between families. Below is an example of 7th century bloodprices from the kingdom of Wessex.

value of a life	silver pennies
thane	6,000
poorer thane	3,000
churl	1,000
slave	0
value of injuries	
broken tooth	20
fingernail	5
fine for refusing to fight for the King	
thane	600
poorer thane	300
churl	150

King Offa AD 757-796

King Offa of Mercia was a ruthless king who spent most of his time invading his neighbours. By AD 780 he had conquered Kent, Surrey, Sussex and Wessex to become the first 'King of the English'. Charlemagne, King of the Franks and the most powerful ruler in Europe, called Offa his 'brother'. He saw Offa and all kings as protectors of the Church. The two Kings traded and offered protection for each other's subjects and exchanged gifts. Offa built the most impressive monument ever constructed in Europe at this time, his famous dyke. He was one of the first Kings to produce silver coins with his image on it and some with his Queen, Cynethryth, in the new wider, thinner style of continental coins.

Offa's Dyke

It is about 180 kilometres long, 7 metres high and 18 metres across with a 2 metre ditch. It stretched the length of the Welsh border, *'from sea to sea'* as one historian wrote. It was longer than the two Roman walls put together and was built to hold back the warring Welsh warlords.

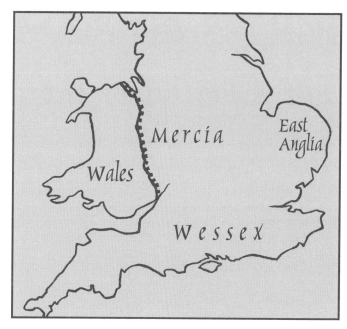

This map shows the position of Offa's Dyke on the border between Wales and Mercia

Did You Know?

Earthworks like Offa's Dyke have been built in Britain since the Bronze Age, but not as big as this one. It would have taken thousands of men to construct the dyke. It is not continuous, because in the north it joins on to another dyke and along its length there are breaks where the ground is naturally impenetrable to invasion. Some stretches show evidence of wood or stone ramparts, built above the turf mound.

PART 3 AD 800-1066
The Coming of the Vikings

'In this year, dire portents appeared over Northumbria. They consisted of immense whirlwinds and flashes of lightning, fiery dragons were seen flying in the air. A great famine followed and a little after that, on 8th June, the ravage of heathen men miserably destroyed God's church on Lindisfarne.' **So says the Anglo-Saxon Chronicle for AD 793.**

This attack on the rich Lindisfarne monastery was one of several raids on English coastal settlements at this time. The monastery was burned, monks slaughtered and treasures stolen. The raiders were the Vikings, which may mean 'sea-borne adventurer' or 'pirate', and referred to the Danish and Norwegian invaders of Northern Europe. These attacks made little impact on Anglo-Saxon society. They only seemed serious because the victims of the raids were monks, who recorded the destruction of Christian places.

English Kingdoms Conquered
However, by the mid 9th century Danish Vikings returned in greater numbers, sometimes with more than 200 ships and thousands of men. They conquered East Anglia, most of Mercia and the great wealthy kingdom of Northumbria. London and the River Thames, with its trading routes to the continent, were also under their control.

Why Did the Vikings Invade?
The Vikings were originally sea-traders whose trading posts in foreign lands often grew into colonies. There had been a population explosion and the Scandinavian farming lands could not support the extra people. Therefore, raids were planned to obtain not just loot and slaves, but also new lands.

The Danelaw
The Danish Vikings under King Guthrum decided to attack the kingdom of Wessex. They surprised its king, Alfred, and he had to flee. At the time there was no regular English army as all of the fighting men were farming. Alfred escaped to the Somerset marshes where he was joined by many warriors.

In AD 878, after a fierce battle, Alfred defeated Guthrum at Edington near Bath. Guthrum agreed to be baptised and withdrew to become King of East Anglia. The Danes signed a treaty with Alfred and agreed to stay in the north and east of England. This area became known as the 'Danelaw'. In AD 886 Alfred recaptured London and rebuilt its walls.

Anglo-Saxon England Changes
In Wessex, Alfred built forts called 'burhs' and this is where we get the word 'borough' from. They grew into thriving towns. The burhs were manned by troops who gave shelter to the local villagers in times of danger. Some were built on old Roman forts, or walled towns, others were completely new. People went to the new towns to buy and sell their produce. Burhs like Southwark, Worcester, Oxford and Winchester became important market centres. Earlier towns had grown on coasts and rivers for trading purposes, but now they were further inland because of the Viking threat. Burhs had their own courts, local governments and tax collectors.

New Neighbours
In the Danelaw, Vikings used their own language, laws and customs, some even married local women. They kept fortified bases. Towns like Norwich, Peterborough, Cambridge and Ely became wealthy through trade. In the countryside many Vikings took over English farms and their strip fields.

Draw a circle and create a design for a Viking or Anglo-Saxon shield. Decorate it with patterns, animals, or metal ornaments. Use tin foil or chocolate wrappers for the metal parts.

King Alfred bakes cakes!
There is a story that when Alfred was fleeing from the Danes, he hid in a cowman's house. The cowman's wife asked him to watch some cakes she was baking in the oven. He was preoccupied and forgot all about the cakes and they burnt. When the woman returned she scolded Alfred, not realising he was her King!

The Vikings had some great nicknames:
Ketil Broken-Nose
Kirstin Red-Eyes
Olaf Hairy-Breeches
Ingrid Starry-Eyes
Eric Blood-Axe
Sweyn Thick-Legs
Olaf Seal-Head
Sigtrygg Silky-Beard
Can you make any up?

The Viking Longship
The average longship carried about 60 men. It was about 25 metres long and in good conditions could travel about 200 kilometres in a day.

Sometimes large hoards of treasure had to be buried to protect it from Viking raids. Some of this treasure has been found and is now in museums. See if you can find five bags of treasure in this picture.

This map shows the area of the Danelaw given to Danish settlers

Sacrificed to Odin!

The pagan Vikings hated the English Christian kings and executed some of them in a gruesome way. One Viking sacrificed two kings to the god Odin using the **'blood-eagle'**. This involved cutting away some ribs from the victim's spine, ripping his lungs out of his back and draping them across his shoulders. They would pulsate like an eagle's wings as the victim slowly died.

King Alfred 'The Great'

Alfred is remembered as the King who burnt some cakes and beat the Danish, but there are many more reasons why he is the only English King to have earned the title 'Great'.

Alfred was born at Wantage in Oxfordshire around AD 849. He was the fifth son of Aethelwulf, King of Wessex. He grew up to become a great warrior, statesman, churchman and scholar. Before he was seven he had twice visited the Pope in Rome. We know a lot about his life because he had a court biographer, a Welsh-born bishop named Asser.

God's Punishment for the English

Alfred believed that the role of king was to be Jesus Christ's deputy on earth and it was his duty to promote Christian standards. He believed that the Vikings had been sent by God as a punishment for not studying the Bible and other books of improvement. So, he set to work to stop any further divine punishment and to strengthen the nation's defences.

Alfred's Solution

Alfred wrote *'the knowledge of Latin was in decay throughout England, but many could read English.'* He wanted people to understand the law and the Bible, so he gathered scholars from the continent to educate the clergy, nobles and judges. At the age of 38 he took advantage of a time of peace to learn to read and write. He translated Latin books into Anglo-Saxon, or Old English, so that more people could read them. He was the only King to write a book until Henry VIII.

New Laws

He set up new laws based on what he considered the best from earlier law codes, placing the Ten Commandments at the beginning of his law book. Many of his laws reflected Christian teaching: *'Judge thou very fairly. Do not judge one judgement for the rich and another for the poor; nor one for the more dear and another for the one more hateful'.*

To protect his kingdom, taxes were used to pay for the building of a network of forts or 'burhs' and a fleet of ships. No other king before Alfred had 'King of the English' written on coinage and he was called this on charters, or legal papers. Alfred himself was the first to use the name 'Angelcynn', or 'English people'. He died in AD 899 having ruled for 28 years.

Food and Feasting in Anglo-Saxon Times

Families baked their own bread made from flour and water, or acorns if there had been a bad harvest. They ate it with cheese made from sheep's milk and drank barley ale, or mead made from fermented honey. In the winter the weaker animals might be slaughtered for food, but usually the poor did not eat meat except during a feast. Feasts took place on special holidays, or at harvest time, when the villagers went to the thane's hall. They ate boar, pork, lamb, beef and venison, which was cut up and eaten using their fingers. Salt preserved the diced meat, or it could be hung from the roof rafters and smoked by the constantly burning fire.

Feasting was an important part of Anglo-Saxon life. As a token gesture of his care, the thane handed out bread to his guests as they arrived. The word 'lord' means 'loaf guardian'. They sat on trestle tables covered in linen cloth. Weapons were hung for decoration and to keep them close at hand in case of a surprise attack. Decorated drinking horns, or in wealthier households glass cone-shaped cups were used, but the contents had to be downed in one go, or passed around and shared because they could not sit them upright. Those who could afford it drank expensive wine from the continent.

What Did They Do at a Feast?

A king or leader might publicly praise and reward his supporters. Guests were welcomed, as they brought news from other places. They could also be a future ally. Gambling with bone dice and board games were popular activities and a version of 'jacks' was played. Story-telling (see page 11) and riddles were very popular.

Women

When a woman married, she was given a 'morning gift', which was money and land if her husband was wealthy, or a brooch, or pots if he was poorer. Most marriages were arranged, but the woman could refuse to marry a man she did not like. She also had the right to leave her husband. Women were less independent than they are today, but some of them owned land they had been given and could become quite powerful.

CHEATS!

Some people cheated! Two dice found in Norfolk were made so that they always came up with a six!

FAVOURITE BOARD GAME

What is your favourite board game?

Design a Board Game

Represent the journey you are making from your Anglo-Saxon homeland to settle in England. Make card counters shaped like warriors and use a dice. Draw a map for the board and add the journey - a series of squares in a winding path. Some of the squares will be blank, others will have hazards, so you will miss a turn, or go back several spaces. Hazards could be bad weather, Romano-British warriors, or Picts attacking, wild animals, other Anglo-Saxons fighting you, famine, the plague, theft, the gods being angry etc. You could have bonus moves for good weather, or help from an ally. Decorate your board with animals, interlaced patterns, ships etc.

Viking Rulers

Alfred and his sons united England. His son Edward brought the Danelaw under English rule and his grandson Aethelstan earned the support of the Welsh and Northumbrian leaders. He defeated the Scots in a decisive battle at Brunanburh, which is near Carlisle.

For a while England enjoyed a period of peace and stability. The Danes were not eager to welcome new Viking settlers in the Danelaw. England had strong defences and the Vikings found easier targets at home, as silver was arriving from Afghanistan.

However, England was growing very wealthy due to the demand from the continent for English wool for the cloth industry. Towns like London and York were growing rapidly and large amounts of silver coins were in circulation. Because of this and as the flow of silver from Afghanistan began to dry up, the Vikings began new raids on English territory. In AD 980 the dragon-carved prows of the longships appeared at Southampton beach.

A Viking King of England
By then England was ruled by Aethelred II, the 'Unready'. The standing army Alfred the Great had created was no more and English defences had fallen into disrepair. Aethelred tried to buy off the new raiders by collecting taxes to pay the Danish 'Danegeld' or 'Danes' gold. This and other attempts at diplomacy did not work. At one point he had to flee to Normandy, but returned only to be defeated by the Danish King Cnut. He became the King of England in 1016 at the age of 21 years. He married Aethelred's Norman widow Emma, Queen of England, to please the English. Aethelred's two sons lived in exile in Normandy. A Viking king was now on the throne.

A Struggle for Power
By now the English Danes were Christians, considering themselves more English than Viking. They even spoke English, although with a Danish accent. Cnut introduced many reforms, such as making Sunday a day of rest from business and amusements. He banned the English Danes from pagan worship. During his reign England enjoyed peace once again. However, one of his reforms was to divide England into four parts, Northumbria, East Anglia, Mercia and Wessex, appointing powerful Earls to rule over them. This was to have dire consequences.

When Cnut died at the age of 40 years there was a lot of confusion, as different people wanted to rule. Queen Emma wanted her Anglo-Saxon sons living in Normandy on the throne. However, Cnut had two Danish sons in England from another wife. It was a pagan custom to have more than one wife. The four powerful Earls were divided between the Danish claim and the Anglo-Saxon claim. Who would win?

King Cnut Goes to the Seaside
There is a story that Cnut's advisors flattered him and told him that he could do anything. He could even stop the sea coming in! Cnut was tired of their flattery, so he had his throne carried to the seashore. When the tide came in, he got his feet wet like anybody else, proving to his flatterers that they were wrong.

Edward 'The Confessor'
Cnut's Danish sons reigned for a time, but they died and ended the reign of Viking kings. In AD 1043 Aethelred's Anglo-Saxon son Edward was crowned King by the Archbishop of Canterbury, restoring the Anglo-Saxon line to the throne. Edward was more French than English, having been educated in Normandy. He surrounded himself with Norman advisors and thought the English were uncultured. He gave land to Normans and appointed Norman Bishops. Westminster Abbey was built in the new Norman style, 'Romanesque'. Edward was also middle-aged and unlikely to produce an heir to the throne. He was more interested in church life than protecting England. During his reign the navy was vastly reduced, which was a significant factor in 1066.

Who Would be the Next King?
Harold, Earl of Wessex, was the popular choice for the English throne. He had quarrelled with his brother Tostig, Earl of Northumbria. Tostig allied himself with *King Harald of Norway,* who was related to Cnut and had claims on England, but nobody wanted Vikings on the throne again. Then there was *Duke William 'the Bastard'* of Normandy, a relative and also favoured by Edward to be his successor. He had the Pope's support too.

A Witan

The King meeting with his council, or Witan at Winchester. It was made up of nobles from all over England and included Bishops.

Lady Godiva

King Cnut's Earl of Mercia was Leofric. His lady was called Godgifu, or Lady Godiva. The story goes that Lady Godiva wanted to remove the heavy burden of taxes from the people of Coventry, so that they could afford to buy art. She argued with her husband who refused to stop the taxes. Leofric said she had to prove to him how much she really cared for art by riding through the city naked, showing the beauty of God's creation. To his surprise she agreed and the taxes were stopped.

The Norman Invasion

Edward the Confessor died in January AD 1066. He had been more interested in being a good churchman than making England strong. He preferred the French to the English and confusion about his successor was to have catastrophic results.

In almost his last breath, Edward appointed Harold his successor under pressure from his advisors. Harold was the only one of the contenders to the throne who was in England at the time. He hurried to be crowned king. His coronation at Westminster Abbey and Edward's funeral were on the same day!

The Vikings Attack

Meanwhile, King Harald of Norway landed his fleet of 300 ships in the north, joined by Harold's brother Tostig with a Scottish army. Harold marched his army day and night the 310 kilometres to York, which was now under Viking control. It took them just six days. The Vikings thought it would be an easy invasion and had sent many of their men back to their ships. The rest of the Vikings were on their way back to York when Harold surprised them at nearby Stamford Bridge. On 25th September, 1066 both Harald of Norway and Tostig were killed in a decisive victory for the Anglo-Saxon army.

The French Attack!

Three days later William 'the Bastard', Duke of Normandy landed his force of 2,000 cavalry and 5,000 infantry at Pevensey Bay in Sussex. His men erected a wooden fort at Hastings. So, Harold now marched his army south, but not all of his troops went with him. He reached London and gathered 6,000 men, then he marched 90 kilometres to Hastings. On 14th October he deployed his infantry on a hill to counter the threat of the Norman cavalry.

William 'the Bastard'

The Duke of Normandy, known by his unkindly nickname, had a reputation for being a great fighter. After the battle he would be known as 'the Conqueror'. Knights had flocked to him from other parts of France as well as Normandy, hoping that they would be rewarded with English lands.

The Battle

William's army moved fast, taking Harold's tired army by surprise. His cavalry rode along the English line, throwing javelins at them to try and break their shield wall. Next volleys of arrows rained down on the tightly packed English causing heavy losses.

Exact details of the battle are unclear. The Bayeaux Tapestry supports the idea that some of Harold's men were lured off the hill, breaking the shield wall, by fake retreats from the Norman cavalry. Harold's death is also unclear. He may have been hit in the eye with an arrow, just like a quarter of the men on the Tapestry were. He was probably hacked to pieces by Norman knights and was so badly mutilated that only his wife, Edith Swan Neck, could identify his remains.

King William I

William met very little further resistance and was crowned king in Westminster Abbey on Christmas Day. The Duke granted the Anglo-Saxon lands of those who had opposed him to the Normans who had helped him. He was merciless in dealing with any opposition and ensured that no Anglo-Saxons were left in positions of power.

The End of Anglo-Saxon England?

Under Norman rule slavery was replaced by a system. Farmers were tied to their lands under strict obligations to their lords, becoming 'serfs'. The English language was too ingrained to disappear and it was enriched by French words. French became the language of the King and nobility for the next 300 years. The Norman mounted knight, spear under his arm, changed the way the English fought. A system of wooden forts and later stone *keeps* brought a new feature to the British landscape, the castle. William ordered the first census of the livestock, contents and people. It was so thorough that people feared the 'Day of Judgement' had arrived, which is why it was called the 'Domesday Book'. At the time of the census there were two million people living in England. Overall England did not undergo a revolution, more of a development and it was now firmly part of Europe.

The Battle of Hastings

Norman knights hurl javelins at the English shield wall to try and break it up

The Bayeaux Tapestry

It is not actually a tapestry at all, but embroidery. It was probably produced by Anglo-Saxons under the supervision of the Bishop of Bayeaux, half-brother of William. It is over 70 metres long and half a metre high and it tells the story of the Battle of Hastings and the events which led up to it.

Create a tapestry from A4 paper. Tell your life story, putting in only the most important events. Decorate the top and bottom with borders and allow room in your design to write a few words which tell viewers what each scene is about.

A Hot Coronation!

When William was crowned he was acclaimed king in French and English by those gathered in Westminster Abbey. His soldiers outside thought the noise was the start of a rebellion, so they set fire to the houses around them!

Did You Know?

The King of France gave Viking pirates an area of Northern France called Normandy to settle in. He wanted a buffer state to stop any further Viking invasions. Four generations later, William became its ruler upon his father's death. The Normans were actually Viking, not French!

Giant Anglo-Saxon Word Search

H	B	G	A	N	O	R	M	A	N	S	E	A	S	L	A	V	E	O	R
L	T	A	O	F	S	W	E	S	T	S	T	O	W	O	H	T	V	S	B
T	R	A	Y	T	E	R	L	A	V	I	D	O	G	Y	D	A	L	H	E
A	E	U	B	E	U	O	L	R	A	V	I	D	A	L	T	P	U	E	O
E	M	A	H	E	A	M	I	M	E	R	C	I	A	K	I	S	D	A	W
R	P	L	E	C	T	U	S	N	E	Q	U	W	I	M	P	E	U	H	U
G	E	S	O	N	A	N	X	T	O	R	D	N	I	S	B	E	A	S	L
E	R	U	U	M	S	V	A	T	P	E	G	M	C	T	N	S	L	I	F
H	O	T	A	N	G	L	O	S	A	X	O	N	S	R	O	E	L	T	A
T	R	T	F	D	S	L	A	R	R	P	N	E	I	P	C	Y	E	I	I
D	C	O	F	S	A	L	G	T	A	L	E	S	I	I	A	R	V	R	R
E	L	N	O	E	C	N	H	X	Q	I	A	S	R	O	S	G	I	B	D
R	A	H	G	A	I	U	E	A	V	I	Q	P	T	M	O	N	A	O	A
F	U	O	N	K	R	S	S	I	A	L	D	S	U	R	L	O	S	N	H
L	D	O	I	N	S	H	K	C	O	O	E	C	E	T	Y	I	A	A	E
A	I	E	K	E	E	I	T	U	O	H	A	B	I	S	K	N	O	M	R
G	U	I	W	R	N	S	T	L	Q	A	E	S	E	A	A	A	E	G	O	U
N	S	N	E	G	U	S	B	T	M	T	H	A	N	E	S	L	N	R	N
I	E	S	S	C	T	U	R	D	A	R	K	A	G	E	S	A	I	S	E
K	C	E	N	N	A	W	S	H	T	I	D	E	M	N	J	U	T	E	S

Pagan	Sutton Hoo	Beowulf	St Bede	Monks
Runes	Lady Godiva	King Alfred the Great	Edith Swan Neck	Thanes
Churl	Dark Ages	Normans	Bloodprice	West Stow
Slave	Mercia	Vikings	King Offa	Bayeaux Tapestry
Wessex	Anglo Saxons	King Raedwald	Jutes	Romano British

22